T0129933

You Can't Just
Snap out of It

You Can't Just Snap out of It

A Journey from Depression to Healing

Patricia Weatherford

authorHOUSE®

AuthorHouse™
1663 Liberty Drive
Bloomington, IN 47403
www.authorhouse.com
Phone: 1 (800) 839-8640

Published by AuthorHouse 05/18/2015

ISBN: 978-1-5049-1076-7 (sc)
ISBN: 978-1-5049-1075-0 (e)

Library of Congress Control Number: 2015907021

Print information available on the last page.

Any people depicted in stock imagery provided by Thinkstock are models, and such images are being used for illustrative purposes only. Certain stock imagery © Thinkstock.

This book is printed on acid-free paper.

Table of Contents

Dedications and Acknowledgements

First and foremost, I would like to dedicate this book to my God who was really the author of this book and to my loving husband, George Weatherford, who has supported me and sustained me for the last 46 years of marriage. Without him I would not be here today. Secondly, I would like to acknowledge my three children, Bill Weatherford, Christie Weatherford - Trickey and Julie Weatherford - Brown who have always been there for me and who have been my greatest cheerleaders. My grandchildren, Hunter and Jacob Brown and Madeline and Olivia Tassin have been my greatest source of joy during my darkest hours. What a blessing they are!

My dear mother, Dorothy Rice, who is no longer with me, was also one of my biggest supporters. She use to tell me all the time that she wished she could have taken my pain away. She was my best friend.

I would like to thank my sister-in-law, Georgia Morel, who helped in the editing of this book in its early stages and Mike Valentino who continued with the editing in the later stages.

I would also like to express my gratitude to my friends who were always there for me, you know who you are, and who called and came to see me even when I was not very good company.

To my dear friend, Vickie King, who wrote the Forward to my book. You did such a beautiful job.

To Dr. Susan Uhrich, my psychiatrist, who tried everything in her power to help me and who was so compassionate and kind to me.

To Lenore Hervey whose photograph I used for the cover of my book and to Andy Perrin who designed my book cover. Thank you, I absolutely love it.

Lastly, I would like to thank a 13 year old girl, Eva Curnutte, who came up with the title for my book.

Foreword

If you have chosen this book to read it is by no accident. You may be a victim of depression or know someone who lives with this devastating mental illness. Yes, that's right! Mental Illness! No one wants to claim that diagnosis and the stigma behind it. It's high time we drop the stigma, and reference it as though one may have diabetes, cancer, or any other catastrophic disease. Depression is a chemical imbalance in the brain, so it is also a physical illness. Reading this informative book will give people courage to find solutions to this ever-increasing global disease. You are not alone. People from the United States and every continent are downing antidepressants like M&M's.

Flashback to the 1960s when I first met the newlyweds, Patricia Rice Weatherford and her husband George. Pat was a striking brunette with a Coca-Cola bottle figure, and George was Hollywood handsome. Being observant and perceptive, I witnessed a real sadness in those big brown doe eyes of Pat's. I thought, "Why should a beautiful 21 year old bride be so unhappy?" Her lifelong battle with depression was just beginning to rear its ugly head. Thus began my 46 year-old friendship with my greatest of friends, Pat and George.

> Pat holds a Bachelor of Science degree and a Master's degree in Secondary Education with a minor in Special Education. She taught for 30 years. In her book, "You Can't Just Snap Out Of It", she will attempt to share the knowledge, resources, and her life's journey with depression. Having suffered for the better part of her life, I would proclaim her as an "expert" in that area, for she has lived it and paid her dues.

I highly recommend this book for its contents will benefit you, the reader, by providing knowledge, awareness and especially the hope that any sufferer seeks when confronted with this illness.

As a friend to Pat, I was able to relate because I, too, suffer from depression. Therefore, I never judged her but rather encouraged and empathized with her during her dark days. One day I realized she had reached the depths of hell when she told me that she wished she would be diagnosed with cancer. Then she said, "That would be the end to my depression." I knew how serious the situation had become and became concerned for her life.

Pat finally took "the bull by the horns" and began an Internet search for treatment options. One of the options was becoming a part of a clinical trial for a new drug, actually a nasal spray, that could knock out depression in a couple of uses. This drug is on a fast track to becoming a reality due to the high number of suicides that are taking place in our world today. Pat tried to get in on this study but was denied because of her age. She also tried TMS therapy recommended by her psychiatrist, Dr. Susan Uhrich, but that did not work.

> So go ahead. Read on and discover a life story of trials, challenges and victory. This is the story of one courageous woman who fought to conquer and live a life of peace and joy and to possibly help others on this long, dark, and lonely journey of depression. In essence, this was a God-inspired book because depression's

tentacles penetrate deep within the very depths of the soul.

Vickie Joy LeBlanc King BA Degree, University of Louisiana at Lafayette

Introduction

One night I was laying face down on the floor before the Lord thanking Him and giving Him praises because I had just come out of a six month depression and was very grateful that I was once more "alive" again.

All of a sudden I felt His overwhelming presence. I stayed in that position for quite a while and then I finally got up off the floor. It was late so I went to my bedroom but couldn't sleep. My husband was snoring so I decided to sleep in my grandchildren's room in the back of the house. The minute I laid my head on the pillow God touched my heart. He said that He wanted me to write a book on what it both feels and looks like to live in a depressed person's body. He wanted me to help people understand this debilitating illness so that they could become more empathetic and supportive toward their loved ones, friends, co-workers and depressed people in general.

As I was lying down I began writing the book in my head. My thoughts were coming fast and furiously. I got up and went to my computer and began typing. My fingers were flying over the keys with no hesitations and when I had finished I had typed six and a half pages of thoughts. I had not slept the entire night.

For over thirty years I have suffered from Clinical Depression. It started in my late thirties and each year I would have a bout with it that would last for at least three to four months.

What is Clinical Depression? It is a depression so severe as to be considered abnormal and is usually caused by a chemical imbalance in the brain. It is different from Situational Depression, which usually occurs in a person who has suffered from a traumatic event like the loss of a child or spouse, or from a divorce, loss of a job, or an illness.

Depression is a brain disease. It is not a character defect or personality disorder. It is usually inherited and passed down from one generation to the next. My paternal grandmother had it, as did my dad, my oldest son, my daughter and firstborn grandson.

My purpose in writing this book is not to explore the cause, effects and symptoms of this disease. There has already been enough written about depression. What I hopefully want to do is to help you understand what life is like when you suffer from this debilitating illness. It is hard to explain depression if one has never experienced it. I have tried to explain it to my family and friends but they just don't understand. My own husband who has lived with me for the last forty-six years and who has seen me cry a bucketful of tears doesn't understand what it feels like.

Over the years I have taken just about every antidepressant on the market. They would work for a while and then they stop. The older I got the worse the depression got and the longer it would last. Finally, it reached the point where none of the medications I was taking were working for me anymore.

That is why it is so important that this book be written. Depression can sink a person to the point where you see no hope and you just want to end it all. I don't consider suicide as an option, but I do feel that I now have a purpose in my life and that is to write this book. And so I begin.

When It First Began

I was twenty-three years old when I experienced my first depression. I was in my third year of teaching full time at a local high school and I thought I could take on the world. That was exactly what I did. I was senior class advisor in charge of graduation, head of the P.E. Department and Girls'Athletics and also in charge of a 120 member intramural program after school as well as girls' track coach. On top of this I had a husband, son and twin daughters to care for. I basically was a crazy person and didn't even know it. By the end of the school year, I couldn't think straight. I had to get someone to help me with my end of the year school records. I walked around in circles all day long, not knowing what was wrong with me. I finally went to see someone who answered that question for me. My therapist told me that I had experienced a complete and total burnout. She told me if I didn't start taking care of myself and have some kind of balance in my life that this would most likely happen again.

For you see, I was a perfectionist who could only rely on myself to get the job done right and that attitude was my downfall. Whatever job I had to do I would go above and beyond the call of duty to make sure it was done right. My therapist told me I needed to eat right, get plenty of sleep, exercise, learn to meditate and have fun. The only problem was I couldn't sit still long enough to meditate.

The next time I experienced another depression was when I was twenty-seven. Something traumatic happened to me during that year that caused me to go into a very dark place. I stayed that way on and off for the next three years. During that time I began taking Valium which was prescribed for me by my doctor. The flip side was that Valium took the edge off and helped me with anxiety. The down side was that I became addicted to the medication and began taking more and more to relax. Finally one day my husband took my bottle of pills and threw them down the toilet. I wanted to kill him. I didn't know that I was supposed to get off this medication gradually. I just went "cold turkey" and could have died from doing so.

In 1987 on Christmas Day, we were driving to my husband's sister's home when all hell broke out in the car. My children were now teenagers and all I can remember was everyone yelling at everyone with me yelling the loudest. When we arrived at my sister in law's house, I told my family that I was going home and that they could find a ride home. When I got back to my house I went straight to my bedroom, undressed, put my nightgown on, got into bed and proceeded to pull the covers over my head. I began sobbing uncontrollably and when I finished I had decided that I could no longer keep living this way. There was something wrong with me and I needed to find out what it was. With the help of my husband and my school principal I checked myself into a facility that dealt with depression and co-dependency. Since I had already dealt with my addiction to Valium I had to cope with other issues. It turns out that I had a lot of pent up rage toward my father for growing up in an alcoholic home. My father use to tell my sister and me all the time that children were to be seen but not heard. We were never allowed to express any of our feelings, so I just stuffed them until they started coming out sideways at my husband and children in the form of rage. Two things happened to me while I was in the hospital. First, I found out that I was borderline bi-polar and was put on Lithium and secondly, I had the opportunity to deal with my anger issues toward my father.

When I returned home things got a lot better. My relationships with my husband and children greatly improved and I felt like a "normal human being." The medication that I was taking leveled me out and I no longer had racing thoughts. I was very grateful that I had gone into the hospital to find out that I had a chemical imbalance in my brain and it wasn't my fault.

When I was into my fifties I noticed that my depressions were lasting longer and that they were more severe. I was seeing different psychiatrists but not one seemed to know the right medication that would keep me from spiraling downward. At one point I was hospitalized because I was taking so much medication that I began doing bizarre things. That was in September of 2010. I went in to a hospital against my will and my stay was very stressful. It affected me so much that my blood pressure went out of control and I completely lost my voice. I told my husband that if he did not get me out of this hospital I was going to die. My psychiatrist released me against her better judgement, but I did not care because I was getting out of there. I told my husband if he ever did that to me again I would divorce him.

The depression continued through 2011 to 2014. I thought that if I had to live the rest of my life like this that I wished God would take me either through an accident or a terminal illness. God had something different in mind. I was at the end of my rope when my psychiatrist brought me into her office and told me about TMS therapy. TMS stands for Trans-Cranial-Magnetic Stimulation which is a non drug form of therapy used to treat adults whose medications no longer work for them. If a person suffers from long-term depression it is believed that there are no longer neurotransmitters left in the brain to carry medications where they need to go. That is why my medications were no longer working for me. So I started TMS therapy on March 12, 2013. I went every day for four and a half weeks and by April 24th I was completely out of my depression and never felt better in my entire life. In seven months I was back into another depression. I felt hopeless.

It's In Our Genes

Depression is a genetic disease that is passed on from one generation to the next. My paternal grandmother had it, as did my dad, my oldest son, one of my twin daughters and now my oldest grandson.

My grandmother was a very talented woman who sang and played the piano for the Mormon Tabernacle Choir. My father told me that she used to scream at him and his sister all the time. She also lived with depression. In those days they did not know what bi-polar disorder or depression was much less how to treat it. So she just suffered in silence. My father was more clinically depressed than he was bi-polar.

I have such fond memories of my father when I was young. I can remember how we used to go to the drive-in movies on Friday nights. My mother would pop popcorn and we would bring an ice chest full of drinks. On Sundays, we would all go to church together and then drive out to this beautiful lake where an old cruise ship was docked and fed the ducks. Afterwards we would all go to Borden's Ice Cream shop for ice cream. We could order whatever we wanted and I always got a banana split. Those were the good old days.

I have no good memories after that. We moved to a small town so that my dad could go to work for my mother's father. My mother begged him not to go work for her father, but he thought he could advance in my grandfather's company. That turned out not to be the case. My grandparents did not like my father because he was not "one of them." My mother was a Southerner and my father was from the North. They met while he was in the service. My grandparents treated my father as an outsider and it hurt him very much. He began to suffer from depression at around the same time I did, around my late thirties or early forties.

My dad was an extremely intelligent man and highly talented as an artist and sculptor. He was also a very tortured soul. I see that now, but I didn't see it while I was growing up. He began drinking to ease his pain and things got really bad around our house. He became a very angry man and he used to unleash those feelings on me.

I was scared to death of him and stayed away from my house as much as possible.

I don't know what I would have done if I had not had my mother. We were very close and a lot of times she would get in the middle of my father and me. Then she would be the one to incur his wrath. I couldn't understand why my father could not just "snap out of" his depression. Now I fully understand.

My daughter is now 40 years old. She suffers from bi-polar depression. Bi-polar disorder is a disease whereby a person suffers from extreme highs and lows of personality, fluctuating between mania and depression. There are several good medicines on the market today, which help with this disease, but the bad thing about that is that the medicine works so well and the patient feels so good he becomes convinced he is cured and stops taking the meds. Then they climb way up there and come crashing down. My daughter and I are both guilty of this and have suffered untold misery as a consequence. You would think that we would have learned our lessons, but that is the usual pattern that occurs.

My oldest son is now beginning to suffer from clinical depression. He is forty-three. I hate this disease. Sometimes I ask myself "Why us?" And then there is my oldest grandson who began experiencing depression at the age of eleven.

My grandson and I are quite close. One day we were sitting on the couch talking and he looked very down. He knew that I suffered from depression so he asked me what it felt like. I told him about the symptoms and he said that he thought he was depressed. My heart broke at that point and I thought, damn, this horrible disease. I hate it! The only good thing that came from knowing was that I would be able to help him. I took him to his family doctor, who put him on an antidepressant. His mood improved quickly.

It is hard to deal with the fact that my grandson at age eleven is already on an anti-depressant. It is easier to bear, though, considering the consequences if he was not being treated.

Mental illness is a difficult thing to talk about. It is easier to understand a physical illness like diabetes or heart disease. Mental illness is just now coming out of the shadows where people are starting to understand and one reason for that is because of all the suicides that are happening in our society today. This is the result of people who suffer from untreated mental illness. Look at all of the shootings that have taken place in our schools, at movie theaters, shopping malls, etc. Many of these are likewise the result of tragically untreated mental illness. Hopefully, in our lifetime, they will discover a cure for depression, bi-polar disorder, schizophrenia and other related conditions that plague our world today.

Chapter 3

A Day In The Life Of

What does it feel like and look like to be in a depressed person's body? This question goes to the heart and soul of this book. Unless you have suffered with depression yourself it is hard to explain it to others. I have a friend who also suffers from this disease and there have been many times that she and I have shared our feelings with each other. It was so nice to hear from that person that she understood what I was going through.

Normally I am a very outgoing person. I love to travel, sing in the choir at my church, play games of any kind, especially bridge, go camping, work in my yard and take care of my grandchildren. My grandchildren mean everything to me. I enjoy their company and they enjoy mine. We have lots of fun together. I also have a wonderful group of friends who love and support me in all that I do. We have been in a Bible study for the past six years and have shared the deepest parts of our lives with one another. We also do service work together and travel at least once or twice a year to Florida and other places.

My best friend and biggest supporter has always been my husband. We met while in college, married and began our lives together in the same town that we still live in today. My husband has always been my rock. He gave me a rare gift and that was his unconditional love for me. Over the years this would prove to be what sustained me in my darkest hour. Without him, I might not be here today.

So what is it like to suffer with this debilitating illness? Well, I can tell you one thing. It is not fun!

My last depression was so severe that I literally did not get out of bed for the first three months. I was on heavy-duty medication and all I did was sleep. When I would awake in the morning I would get out of bed, go to the kitchen, get two more sleeping pills and go back to bed. I wanted to knock myself out so I wouldn't have to feel the dread of facing the day.

When I finally did drag myself out of bed I would go into the living room and zone out in front of the TV. It was the only thing that gave me comfort during the entire time of my depression.

People would call me and I wouldn't answer the phone. I would take it off the hook so that the phone would not wake me. When I was awake I let the phone go to voice mail. My family and friends were worried about me but I found it very difficult to carry on a conversation with anyone. Even though I did not answer the phone what I want to say is don't be afraid to call your loved one and let them know that you are thinking about them. It always helped me to know that people cared enough to call even though I was unable to talk to them.

My grandchildren wanted to come over and spend the night but I refused. I couldn't stand the commotion and noise. When my husband talked me into having them because he missed them so much I wouldn't even get out of bed to feed them in the morning. All I wanted was for them to leave so that I could be left alone. I felt so guilty about those feelings. I thought what a terrible person I am. I love my grandchildren but during those times that I was depressed I just could not handle being around them.

My grandson was failing math for the year at school. I taught math to learning disabled children when I was teaching and I was very good at it. I told his parents that if he could come and live with me for a while, that I would see to it that he passed.

He started doing much better and raised his grade from an F to a C. I was able to help him with no problem because I happened to be doing well at the time.

I never knew from one day to the next how I was going to be. I could be doing great one day and the next day sink to the depths of hell. It would happen that fast!

The next time I needed to tutor my grandson for his high stakes test at the end of the school year I couldn't because I had once again fallen into a depression. I tried to but when I opened the math book I couldn't think. I just sat at the table and cried. I felt worthless and of no use to anyone.

My twelve year old granddaughter and I are very close. She spends almost every weekend at my house and we are soul mates. She is very athletic and plays basketball better than most boys her age. In fact, when she attended a basketball camp they divided the kids into groups according to their age levels and she ended up playing with the high school group. Two semi-pro basketball players approached me after the camp and asked if they could work with her on a one-on-one basis. They thought she had a lot of talent.

I say this about her with much pride because I, too, was a pretty good basketball player in my day, making the All-State team three out of the four years I played. I also played on the very first women's basketball team at my college. I say this not to brag but to explain our bond.

She also plays softball and always asked for me to go to her games. If I was not in a depression I would attend but if I was I wouldn't go. I wanted to go and sometimes I would tell her that I was going but I would not show up. She was always very understanding about it. I would apologize to her and she would just say to me, "That's okay, Mimi."

One day in the car she knew I wasn't doing well. In fact, I started to cry and she just looked at me and said, "Mimi, you are my best friend and I will always be there to take care of you." Those words are forever engraved on my heart and make me smile every time I think about them.

My friends and I get together for "game day" once a month. It was my turn to host it at my house so I decided to go ahead and have it. We were all in the kitchen seated around the table playing Mexican Train. Everyone was laughing and having a great time except me.

I felt like I was on the outside looking in. I wanted so much to be part of the group but I felt so alone, like I was locked up inside myself. When everyone left I sat down and cried. I was so overwhelmed from being around a lot of people. These were my close friends but I just could not handle it. The worst part about it was that I would beat myself up so badly. Why couldn't I have fun like everyone else? What is wrong with me?

One thing I definitely realized was that I could not be around large groups of people when I was depressed. One person at a time was all that I could handle.

My husband did not demand a lot from me when I was "down" but one day he asked me if I would make a pot of spaghetti. I told him that I would but the very thought of it overwhelmed me. I know that sounds ridiculous and I would ordinarily do it with no problem but I just had no energy. The thought of it exhausted me.

Just the thought of getting dressed and going to the store was too much for me. When I got to the store I wandered around trying to think of what I needed to make the spaghetti. It took me a half-hour to pick up five items. Then I would drive home and have to cook it. It took everything I had just to make something that simple.

One day I was having lunch with my friends. I had just finished my TMS Therapy and was completely out of my depression. I shared with them the story about the spaghetti and I think for the first time they understood what depression did to me. They could not believe how much effort it took for me to do something as simple as to make spaghetti. I think at that moment they all finally "got it."

I consider myself to be a very spiritual person. I grew up in a Catholic family, attended an all girl Catholic school and have attended mass regularly all my life. I also pray every day first thing in the morning.

One of the things I love to do is sing in the choir and have done so for the past twenty-five years. When I get depressed, however, I can't pray or sing. What used to give me so much comfort and peace no longer did. I felt so empty inside all I could do was tell God, "I offer up all my pain and suffering to you, Lord." If I had to suffer I might as well make it count for something but I did not always do that in the beginning.

In fact, I used to get angry with God. Why did He make me suffer so much? I was a good person, I thought. Was He trying to teach me a lesson that I needed to learn? These were the questions I kept asking myself throughout the years. It wasn't until a few years ago that I learned that I needed to praise and thank Him for my suffering. So I started doing that and while it didn't take away my pain or lessen it, offering it up made me feel better.

I hope that I have helped you see more clearly what a person goes through when they've fallen into a deep depression. If you can understand the disease you can be more empathetic toward the person who is suffering.

Chapter 4

The Pain It Causes

Depression hurts everyone. When I think of the pain it causes my husband I wish I could die. I don't like being a burden to anyone and yet every time I go through another depression my husband has to go through it, too. When he sees me crying he wishes he could help me, but he can't. It absolutely kills him. It makes him want to run out of the house, get in his car and drive as far away as possible.

My daughters both suffer with me when I get depressed. They call me almost every day to check on me. I recently enjoyed a weekend in New Orleans with one of my daughters and she told me that she treasures the time she spends with me when I am not in a depression. We have so much fun together.

Normally, I love life. I try to live each day like it was going to be my last. Living with depression I never know how much time I will have before I have to go back into that dark, lonely place. So life takes on a totally new meaning for me. I try to cram as much quality time as I can into every day.

My grandchildren miss me when I am depressed. One day I am the fun-loving Mimi who is always doing things with them, going to their games and spending time with them. Then the next day I am in my cocoon and not available to them.

My son also calls me to see how I am doing. He, too, has experienced bouts with depression so he understands. I seem to always start crying when I talk with him on the phone. I don't know why, maybe it's because he does understand.

My friends and other family members have trouble dealing with this disease. They see the normal me who is very involved with everything and they see the depressed me who won't even answer their phone calls. None of them understand this illness because none of them have experienced it.

So the pain that is caused from one suffering with depression is far reaching. It affects everyone who comes in contact with the individual. That is why it is so important to understand this disease so that you can be more supportive, loving and compassionate.

Chapter 5

Snap Out Of It

There are all kinds of things people say to you when they know that you are depressed. They mean well, but they simply don't understand the disease. Most people go through their entire lives never having experienced it. Some will experience Situational Depression at some time in their lives. Others are living with someone who is depressed or know people in their life with this terrible disease. Knowing what to say and not to say is very important, which is one of the primary reasons why I am writing this book.

One of the things people used to say to me is, "snap out of it." If I could have just snapped my fingers and immediately gotten out of my depression I would have been snapping my finger until they fell off.

Another piece of advice I was given was, "push yourself." I couldn't even get out of bed in the morning much less push myself. Depression takes away everything from a person. It takes away your drive to do things, your concentration, your ability to think straight, and your joy. It takes away who you are as a person. All of the things that I hold near and dear to my heart I don't seem to be able to do when I'm depressed, like praying, singing in the choir or working in my yard.

"Get out of yourself and go help someone," is something else that was said to me. "It will make you feel better," they said. Well, that's the truth. Helping others does make you feel good inside. I am always helping others but when I'm depressed it is very difficult to reach out to others in need. I am so needy myself during that time that I can't think about anyone else. That may sound selfish but it is the nature of the disease.

"Go to the gym and exercise," is something I hear all the time. When I am not depressed I go to the gym at least four times a week. I love to exercise and I have done it all my life. However, when I'm depressed I don't feel like doing anything. Put me in front of the TV all day where I can just zone out is about all I can do. Anything else is just too exhausting.

One person told me that a client of hers took her by the shoulders, shook her and said, "Get a grip!"

Then she asked her why she was going to a psychiatrist. "All they do is put you on a lot of meds you don't need."

All of this advice came from people who meant well. They just don't understand the disease of depression. If I can do one thing in writing this book it is to help people understand so that they can be more compassionate toward the person who is suffering from this debilitating illness.

Chapter 6

Situational Depression Vs. Clinical Depression

What is the difference between the two? Situational depression is caused by life's unfortunate circumstances. This is someone who has suffered a tragedy like losing a child, a spouse, experienced divorce, or lost a job or anyone who has had to face a serious health issue like cancer. It can be severe but in most cases it is not permanent. It is not a disease.

With clinical depression you can be fine one day and the next day plunge into the depths of hell. It can come on that fast. It's like a light switch that can go off and on at a minute's notice. This type of depression is a brain disease. It is caused from a chemical imbalance in the brain, is usually inherited and can display symptoms of suicide at times.

The symptoms of situational depression do not usually include thoughts of suicide. It is not nearly as debilitating as clinical depression but both types should be treated by a proper medical professional. There are many good and effective meds out there with a seventy percent effectiveness rate and little or no side effects.

There is also the aforementioned TMS Therapy. Help is available for the depressed person. One need not suffer in silence.

I recently read an article in a magazine about a man who suffered from clinical depression. He said that he would rather have boiling water poured over his genitals and thighs a hundred times than to live with severe depression. That left a very strong impression on me. It is how I feel at times with my months and months of living with this horrible disease. I always say that I would rather suffer from any physical disease like cancer than to suffer with clinical depression.

Chapter 7

From A Caretaker's Point Of View

I am writing this chapter to give the reader some insight as to what a caretaker does. I hope it will give some perspective as to what I do for my wife and myself. I am not an expert on caregiving nor do I purport to be, but I have been at it for thirty-five plus years and have learned through experience.

I was married on December 28, 1968 to the lady of my dreams. She was young, vibrant, beautiful, smart, educated, and full of life. I often thought of how lucky I was to have such a lady for my wife. I always thought that she was smarter than I and therefore I tried to impress her so I could come up to her level.

I grew up in a small town, was an athlete, and joined the Marine Corps out of high school. I then went to college and obtained my BA and MA degrees. That is where I met my wife. We were married and we set out to be successful in life.

I have always been a person who believed in hard work and that almost anything can be fixed if I try hard enough. I would learn over time that some things cannot be fixed and there are some things I cannot control.

In my younger days I had no idea what depression was. I had never experienced it myself, or been around anyone who suffered from depression. Death of a family member or a close friend was hard to bear but I got over it in time.

Early on in my marriage I heard about depression. I would say to my wife, "Let's go and see your mom and dad on Sunday."

She would reply, "I need to call my mom and see if it is ok." I did not quite understand this but went along anyway. She called one time and said we could not go over because her father was depressed. My mother-in-law protected him while he was in a depression. My ignorant response was, "Depressed about what?" I had no clue what depression was. I would find out later.

After a number of years of marriage my wife was teaching physical education at a local high school. She was also head of her department and in charge of graduation for 300 plus students, as well as numerous clubs and activities for the school.

She had three children and me to deal with at home. When the school year ended she experienced a complete burnout and became depressed for the first time in her life.

Being the way I was I simply told her it was temporary and she just needed a break. The depression lasted for eight months! I did not understand what was going on. It then seemed like in the fall of every year the depression would return. I still did not understand what was going on and tried to fix her. I would tell her that she had a beautiful family and everyone loved her and she should realize that. I thought this would help her "snap out of it". I would also say to her, "Go to the gym and get some exercise." I thought this would help her. I blamed myself and asked her if it was something I had done wrong. I asked the question, "Do you still love me?" It was not about me or the family. It was a disease that I had trouble understanding. I still thought I could fix it like I did everything else. I was wrong!

In 1987 we were going to my hometown for Christmas. Her depression was so bad that she left us at my sister's home and drove back to our home. She spent Christmas by herself sobbing uncontrollably. That is when she realized that she needed help and checked herself into a hospital.

She was never short of courage. She was diagnosed with severe chronic depression and put on medication. After a few weeks we saw much improvement. I thought, well this is it, she is cured. I was wrong again! She would either quit taking her medication or the medication would need to be adjusted. A doctor friend told me that was common. He said as soon as they feel better they quit taking their medication. They don't want to admit that they have a mental disease.

Each year the depression would get more and more severe. Each year it would last longer and longer. She had to retire from teaching after thirty years because she could not function for the entire year.

She once walked to the parking lot at her school to find out that she had left her car running with the radio on for hours. That's when she decided to retire. Often when I return home from my office I would find her car with the trunk and driver's door open and she was inside sleeping. I simply closed them and said nothing.

For 40 years I have been learning to deal with her depression. First and foremost, I have learned that I cannot fix it. It is a disease and there is nothing I can do to make it go away.

How many days have I gotten out of bed and not turned on any lights. I simply get my clothes out of the closet with the door closed and get dressed in the bathroom.

I am quiet! She is sleeping. How many days have I called home to check on her and I never got an answer. How many days have I left my office to go home to check on her to find her sleeping. I don't know how many times. I can't count that high.

Now my children and grandchildren call home to see if it is ok to come over to our home. I never dreamed it would be that way. Believe me she feels the same way but worse.

I could come home with great news and it would make no difference or put a smile on her face. I could win the lottery and tell her we were going on an around the world cruise and it would mean nothing. Depression is a deep dark hole that seems to have no bottom.

Years ago I would have never dreamed I would be a caregiver. I was selfish, self-centered and really did not think I could take care of anyone. I have changed. I listen to her and love her without condition. I wish she did not suffer from depression but she does. It is not her fault, she has a disease. I will handle it for the remainder of my life or hers. I will always be there for her as I know she would be for me.

Has it caused me grief? Yes it has. Has it caused me to worry? Yes it has. Has it disrupted our lives? Yes it has. Do I have any regrets? Yes I do, only that she has a disease. I would marry her all over again from the beginning. She is a remarkable lady and she is still smarter than me.

With all of this being said I can assure you that I have learned that I cannot fix this disease. I have learned throughout the years that I simply have to be there and love her.

I have had the honor to work in a ministry called "Kairos" a number of times. It is a prison ministry. There are a number of "men teams" that go into a prison and work with prisoners on their spiritual life. The prison I work in is "Angola", the Louisiana State Penitentiary. The average sentence is 90 years. A priest once told me it was a place of "no hope". We are trained to do two things, "listen, listen, love, love". We do not preach.

If ever I could give advice to a caregiver of a person with depression it is to "listen and love". There is nothing else they want from you and there is nothing else you can do.

God has given me a gift. It is her. She is still the beautiful, smart, and wonderful lady she was when we were first married. She is sick and I will be there to take care of her for however long. God's gift has also been to give me humility and understanding. I have learned to be more empathetic of people in general. These are gifts and I am grateful for them.

My wife and I are both spiritual people. We not only go to church but we often pray together while holding hands. The hardest thing I have had to deal with is when she would say, "I just wish God would take me." I know she would never commit suicide because of her strong spiritual beliefs but to hear her say she wishes God would take her hurts me to the core. It also scares me!

Listen and love are the most important things a caregiver can give, but a caregiver must be proactive. I try to take the stress off of everyday life, cooking, shopping, etc. I also try to keep bad news away from her unless it is absolutely necessary. I do things with her. Take her out if she wants to go and so on. Sometimes this takes a gentle push. I have found that playing cards and games that require thinking helps her concentration and she enjoys it and so do I. It is also important as a caregiver to make sure that she sees her doctor on a regular basis and takes her medication on time and not stop taking it. What do I do for myself? Let me assure you that this job can be very lonely. It can bring you down. I do a number of things. I exercise with weights, go fishing and hunting with my grandchildren. We also go camping as a family. My wife is included in many of these things if she is up to it. I will also go on hunting and fishing trips with a few close friends. When I leave her I have my daughters watch her in my absence. I am fortunate to have close friends who I can talk to and they listen. I don't try to hide anything. It is good for me to sometimes "unload my feelings". I am also fortunate to have a man who shares an office with me who is a psychologist. I talk to him and it is free! Then I just take one day at a time and listen and love.

Chapter 8

What About Medications

The one thing I know for sure is that everyone is different, especially when it comes to taking medications. I used to think that if a certain antidepressant worked well for one person it could work well for me. What I found out was that was not the case. Everyone's body chemistry is different and while one medication may work well for one person the same medication may have severe adverse side effects for another person or may not work at all. I have tried every antidepressant on the market. At first it was hit or miss. I would try one for a while and it would work. Then it would stop working and I would try another. This time I would have terrible side effects from the medication and have to stop. Sometimes I was on as many as six or seven different medications at one time.

I walked around like a zombie. Talk about "the walking dead"! I was it.

Some of the side effects from taking these different antidepressants have been weight gain, lack of sexual desire, inability to express emotions, a dulling of the senses, fatigue and many more too numerous to mention. No wonder many people who are suffering from any form of mental illness stop taking their medications. They are stuck between a rock and a hard place. However, this should not interfere with your decision on whether or not to take medications. I personally know three people who have been on the same medication for years and continue to do very well.

Which brings up this subject. What about those who are prescribed medications for various reasons and who are doing great on their medications, but all a sudden think that because they are doing so well they are "cured". Then they stop taking their medications and down they come. That was my story also. I did that many times throughout my lifetime of dealing with depression. A medical doctor told my husband one day that this was the usual pattern. He said they begin to feel real good and then they think they can get off their meds. And thus begins the vicious cycle of on again, off again.

Another thing that I should mention is the cost of drugs related to mental illness. The medicines used to treat depression, bipolar disorder, schizophrenia, psychotic disorders and other related disorders are quite expensive. I have been very fortunate because I happen to have good insurance. There are many people, however, that have only partial insurance or none at all. These are the ones for whom I feel the sorriest. What do they do?

The last thing I would say in closing is to find a good psychiatrist. This is of the utmost importance. During my lifetime I have been through many. Either they didn't interact with me, or they prescribed too many different medications for me at one time, or they just did not help me. The one I have now is amazing. She is kind and compassionate and has knelt down beside me and held me in her arms while I sobbed. You just have to find the one that is a good fit for you and do what he or she tells you to do. A lot of people who are dealing with mental illness try to self-medicate. They either reduce or increase their meds without consulting their doctor or they quit taking their meds altogether. In other words they play doctor. This is not a good practice and will only delay your recovery, or cause serious side effects.

Chapter 9

Famous People Who Suffered From Depression

There have been many famous people who have suffered with severe depression. All of them have one thing in common. They all went on to do great things with their lives.

Isaac Newton was one of the most famous mathematicians of the 17th Century. His greatest mathematical discovery was the gravitational relationship between the earth and the moon. He suffered from several nervous breakdowns in his lifetime and was known for great fits of rage. Some have labeled him with bipolar disorder, which was unknown at the time.

Ludwig van Beethoven, a composer, had bipolar disorder which some have said gave him great creative powers. He wrote many musical compositions when he was in a manic episode including Beethoven's 5th. His most famous works were written during times of loneliness, torment and psychotic delusions.

Abraham Lincoln, 16th president of the United States, suffered from severe and debilitating depression. There were several times when he was suicidal. He was still able to achieve greatness in his lifetime bringing our country through the Civil War and abolishing slavery.

Winston Churchill, Prime Minister of Great Britain, led the world to defeat Hitler in World War II. He suffered from severe depression. He self-medicated himself with alcohol to get through these times, but still made great contributions to society by the sheer determination of his will.

Vivien Leigh, an actress who was made famous for her role in "Gone with the Wind", suffered from severe bouts of manic depression. She was given shock treatments that helped, only to die some years later from tuberculosis at the age of 53.

Other famous people who have had to cope with mental illness during their lifetimes were Leo Tolstoy, Russian author, Charles Dickens, English author, Michelangelo, artist, Dick Clark, entertainer, Irving

Berlin, composer, Marlon Brando, actor, Buzz Aldrin, astronaut, Ernest Hemmingway, Pulitzer Prize winning author and Mike Wallace, of "60 Minutes" fame, to name a few. There are many more that I have not named.

Chapter 10

Final Thoughts

When I turned on the TV on August 11, 2014 and heard that Robin Williams, age 63, had committed suicide due to severe depression, I was deeply saddened.

This is why this book is so timely. Suicide is becoming more prevalent in our society today. Like I said in the beginning of this book, suicide is increasing at a larger percentage than any other form of death in the United States. That is why it is so important to educate people about mental illness. Over 20 plus million people suffer from debilitating depression, bipolar disorder, schizophrenia, and other psychotic disorders.

Lately, much is being written about depression and suicides in the newspapers, on TV, in magazines, on the Internet and other media outlets. Because of the death of Robin Williams, mental illness is once again coming to the forefront. Here was a man who was loved by millions, who made people laugh, and who possessed enormous talent, wealth and fame. He was a great friend to many and was also a great philanthropist. The ironic part about this is that he suffered from severe depression and took his own life as a result of it.

This is why it is so important for everyone to have their eyes wide open and arm themselves with the knowledge of what to look for, the signs and symptoms, of depression. Parents, educators, and people in general should be vigilant and when they see someone suffering from mental illness they should do something about it. Get that person to a professional. There is help out there. No one should have to suffer in silence anymore. That way we can all work together for the greater good and maybe help decrease the number of suicides that are taking place in our world today.

When I read over my book I know that I did not write this. I have never written a book before this one, nor have I ever had a desire to do so. This book was definitely written by the hand of God. I was strictly His instrument. I hope that I have helped you to better understand this illness called depression so that in the future you can be more supportive of the people you love.

I thought this was going to be the end of my story but it really is just the beginning. When I wrote the chapter, "Final Thoughts," I felt that this was going to be the last chapter of my book. With further consideration, I realized that I needed to tell the rest of my story.

Chapter 11

A Message Of Hope

At the beginning of 2014 I started listening to the sermons of Joel Osteen, pastor of Lakewood Church in Houston, Texas. I had read a book that he published and was very impressed with his uplifting message. I had heard that his sermons were broadcast on TV so I started taping them.

At the time, I was in a severe depression that started in October of 2013 and lasted until April of 2014. I remember watching Pastor Osteen for the first time in January of 2014 and I distinctly remember what he said. He pointed his finger out to the audience and said, "2014 is going to be your year, a year of healing, prosperity, joy, success, increase and overcoming obstacles." He said this year was going to be a time for healing, healing from depression, addictions, physical diseases like cancer, our own internal demons, etc.

He said all you have to do is ask, believe that the healing is going to happen, say it out loud, proclaim it to others, and thank God ahead of time like it has already happened.

That day I asked The Lord to heal me from my depression. I told Him that He promised that He would never send us anything more than we could handle. Well, I could not handle going through another six months of depression. I did not want to commit suicide because of my religious upbringing and because I just could not do that to my family. But honestly I knew that I could not hang in there any longer. God had to heal me!

So I kept listening to Joel Osteen and the more I listened the more I believed deep down inside of me that God was going to take this depression from me. I never wavered or looked back. I just kept telling everyone that God was going to perform a miracle within me.

I came out of my six-month depression April 1, 2014 and have never experienced another depression. Every day when I get up I thank The Lord for healing me. My life is now full of joy and peace. In fact, I can't contain the joy that is within me. It runneth over to everyone I come in contact with. I am so grateful. I want to shout to the rooftops what God has done for me like the blind man, Bartemaus, in the Bible when he was healed.

I now know that I have a real purpose in my life and that God is going to take me places I have never been. My message is of hope. He is putting people in my life every day to minister to. The greatest desire of my heart is to be of service to others. That is what I want to spend the rest of my life doing. I am ready to go wherever God takes me.

What I want to say to you, the reader of this book, is that there is hope. You may suffer from mental illness or you might be the caretaker of one who suffers from this very real illness. You may have a friend or co-worker or family member or just know of someone who is suffering terribly from this debilitating disease. They desperately need your understanding, love, support, and compassion. You can make a difference in their life by becoming aware and arming yourself with the knowledge of what the symptoms are so that you can reach out with love to that person.

I want to say further, that even though I believe myself to be healed I have not stopped taking my medications. Medications have helped many people with their symptoms and they, too, are a gift from God. Where would a person who suffers from mental illness be without them. I am definitely not advocating for anyone to get off their meds. I will keep taking mine until I feel deep down that I no longer need them and that may be never.

In closing, I would like to say that I become overwhelmed with tears every time I think of what The Lord has done for me. To be free from depression after suffering for the past 40 plus years is the most wonderful thing that has ever happened to me. There is hope and I am hear to tell you that God is good. Ask, believe, proclaim, and thank Him ahead of time like the healing has already taken place. If it could happen to me it can happen to you. God wants to heal all of us from whatever holds us in bondage. He wants to set us free.

Epilogue

2014 was a great year. I had gone a whole year free of depression and was the happiest I had ever been in my life. Unfortunately, on April 1, 2015, I fell into another deep depression brought on by several stress factors in my life. After dealing with this for over the past 40 years, I know one thing for sure. Stress is the major factor that brings on depression for me. I have to watch myself as far as taking on too many projects when I come out of a depression. I feel so good that my natural inclination is to jump into living my life again. My son tells me all the time that I take on too much. I realize now that I can't do that any longer. I have to take care of myself.

Your question might be how do I feel about my depression coming back when I thought I had been healed? Very disappointed to say the least! Did I experience a healing from God? Yes, I did. I had a full year of joy. That was the longest I had gone depression free in the last 40 years. It was a gift! It also gave me hope in a sense that I knew there was light at the end of the tunnel. I can truly appreciate the good times because I know what the bad times are like.

Am I angry at God? Yes, I am, for the moment, and I have expressed this to Him. I have no problem being angry with my God. It does not mean that I do not love Him. I get angry from time to time with my husband, children, and grandchildren. This has nothing to do with the love that I feel in my heart for them. I feel the same way about my God. I believe He knows this and understands. I love Him with all of my heart and knows He loves me, too.

He gave me a whole year and I am grateful for that. I am not happy that the depression has come back, but I know that it will pass. I still have hope. I am a fighter and I believe that God likes fighters. I will do everything in my power to continue to fight this battle called Depression and I hope I can inspire you to do the same.

About the Author

Patricia Weatherford resides in Lafayette, LA. with her husband, George, three children, four grandchildren, and one step-grandson. She attended Mt. Carmel Academy in New Iberia, LA. and went on to graduate from the University of Louisiana in Lafayette with a Bachelor of Science Degree and a Master's Degree in Secondary Education and a minor in Special Education.

Pat taught school for 30 years. She retired in 2003 because of having to deal with her many bouts of severe depression. For over 40 years she had to suffer with this debilitating disease.

"You Can't Just Snap Out Of It" is about her courageous journey from depression to joy. This book is very timely because of the many suicides that are taking place in our world today.

Printed in the United States
By Bookmasters